We

Don't Die,

We Kill Ourselves

How to Defeat

The Top Ten Killers

By

Cris C. Enriquez, M.D.

DEDICATION

For my wife, Linda, the love of my life, my inspiration and my best friend.

ABOUT THE AUTHOR

Dr. Cris Enriquez is recognized as the only medical doctor with the unique combination of training in four different medical specialties in the following medical institutions: Pulmonary Medicine at Yale University School of Medicine and Medical Center; Cardiology at Baylor University Medical Center and at Carney Hospital; Radiology at the University of Miami – Jackson Memorial Medical Center; and Internal Medicine at the Hospital of St. Raphael. In addition, Dr. Enriquez has been involved in Public Health as director of Continuing Medical Education and TB Control in Ft. Lauderdale, Florida. His medical practice integrates traditional and alternative medicine with emphasis on prevention and reversal of diseases.

He is the co-founder and Medical Director of Rapha Health Institute in Ft. Lauderdale, Florida, and is in the *Who's Who of Medical Specialties of Health and Medicine* of Florida, of the South and Southwestern United States, and of the world.

Dr. Enriquez has received multiple recognition awards from the American Medical Association, and is a popular lecturer through his Rapha Health Seminars. He can be reached at:
Rapha Health Institute
P.O. Box 460640
Ft. Lauderdale, Florida 33346-0640

INTRODUCTION

The significance of the diseases discussed in this book is not merely to point out that they exist or that they can cause havoc in a family's life when a member is afflicted. But, that they can be prevented, and when already present, can be reversed!

The Bible tells us in 3 John 2,

"I wish above all things that you prosper and be in health just as your soul prospers."

This passage clearly tells us that the Lord wants us to succeed and to have divine health. But, the one condition is that our soul should prosper first. This cannot happen without the renewing of our minds (Romans 12:2) so that we have the knowledge, understanding and wisdom that we need so we do not succumb to the temptation of bad health habits and practices.

All diseases are preventable.

All deaths before the age of 120 years are premature deaths.

God says in Genesis 6:3:

"My Spirit shall not strive with man forever, for he is indeed flesh; yet his days shall be one hundred and twenty years."

Medical science has confirmed this also (not that God's Word needs any confirming from anybody or any organization, notwithstanding their august reputation). The only exception to this is if you have already fulfilled the purpose for which you were created.

So why do people die so young?

There are two main reasons:

1)   Disobedience, and

2)   Ignorance.

There are those who know not only how to stay healthy and are proficient on the scriptures, yet continually disregard and disobey these God-given guidelines – much to their detriment.

Then there are those who just do not know what to do or not to do.

To the former, I Samuel 15:23 says,

"For rebellion is as the sin of witchcraft, and stubbornness is an iniquity and idolatry."

To the latter, Hosea 4:6 says,

"My people perish for lack of knowledge."

The key to staying healthy, happy and living a long time is found in Exodus 15:26 which states,

"If you diligently heed the voice of the Lord your God and do what is right in His sight, give ear to His commandments and keep all His statues, I will put none of the diseases on you which I have brought on the Egyptians. For I am the Lord who heals you."

What are these diseases that were put on the Egyptians?

According to the studies made from more than 30,000 excavated Egyptian mummies, they are the same diseases we encounter today such as heart disease, diabetes, arthritis, etc.

Sickness and disease will not only hamper your lifestyle and productivity but they can also be fatal. And dying a premature death without fulfilling one's purpose is doubly tragic.

To those who have been given the gift of medical knowledge, they should take it upon themselves to help and educate the brethren to the perils of ignorance and disobedience, as far as staying healthy and longevity are concerned.

Through God's grace, I have been given the gift of medical knowledge.

Therefore, this book.

Cris Enriquez, M.D.

TABLE OF CONTENTS

Chapter One
 # 1 Cause of death:
 Heart Disease   11

Chapter Two
 # 2 Cause of death:
 Cancer   35

Chapter Three
 # 3 Cause of death:
 Stroke   51

Chapter Four
 # 4 Cause of death:
 Drug Reactions   59

Chapter Five
 # 5 Cause of death:
 Lung Diseases   71

Chapter Six
 # 6 Cause of death:
 Accidents   87

Chapter Seven:
 # 7 Cause of death:
 Diabetes   95

Chapter Eight:
  # 8 Cause of death:
  Alzheimer's Disease   103

Chapter Nine:
  # 9 Cause of death:
  Coronary Artery
  By-pass Surgery   111

Chapter Ten:
  # 10 Cause of death:
  AIDS   119

CHAPTER ONE

1 CAUSE OF DEATH – HEART DISEASE

"The heart is deceitful above all things, and desperately wicked." Jeremiah 17:9

"He who trusts in his own heart is a fool" Proverb 28:26

In ancient times, lovers showed their love to each other by uttering the most important and biggest organ in the body when they whispered sweet nothings to each other. At that time, they thought this organ to be the liver. Saying "I love you with all my liver" was bilious and unromantic, so they mulled over using the skin when they learned it was the largest organ.

"I love you with all my skin" did not go over very well either, so they scrapped that too (notwithstanding Frank Sinatra's version of "I've got you under my skin.") Digging into their anatomical acumen, the ancients realized that the heart was in the middle of the chest and the whole body. They decided it was probably the most important organ; thus, "I love you with all my heart" came into being.

We are so ever thankful for their discovery!

Thankfully, the heart is now the organ of choice of all lovers and people with dreams and vision. In medicine, however, the heart is considered the most treacherous of organs because when it stops working, life ceases. And there is no telling when or where that will happen. It just happens, and, in a great number of times, without any warning or seeming provocation.

Heart attack, medically known as "acute myocardial infarction", is the most common diagnosis among hospitalized patients in virtually all of the industrialized or developed countries, and it also appears to be the number one cause of death in these countries.

It is the # 1 cause of death in the United States.

About 1.5 million people in the United States suffer an acute myocardial infarction every year. One third, or approximately 500,000, die... with about 250,000 dying before they even get to an Emergency Room or hospital.

Sudden death is the very first symptom in 40% of those who die!

Heart attack is the major cause of sudden death anywhere. It becomes more painful and devastating to a family and friends when it happens to a seemingly healthy individual. It is not uncommon to have this happen to a person who had just received a check-up and pronounced fit and healthy. Every 25 seconds someone suffers a heart attack, and in every 45 seconds, someone dies from it.

Of those people that reached the emergency room, 77% died because of diagnostic and treatment errors (as reported in the August, 1996 issue of *Medical Economics*). And, according to studies at Johns Hopkins University, another 5,000 lives are lost every year when patients are admitted to the wrong hospital.

After the initial hospitalization, 1 out of every 25 patients dies within 1 year after a myocardial infarction. For people who are over 65 years of age, the mortality rate is 1 out of 5 at 1 month and about 1 out 3 within one year after an infarction.

WHAT ARE THE SIGNS AND SYMPTOMS OF A HEART ATTACK?

A heart attack can present itself in several different ways:

1.	Death: Sadly, in a lot of people, this is the first symptom of a heart attack. There is no previous history of heart disease or complaints of any kind. Most heart attacks happen on Monday mornings between 8 and 9 a.m.. This is presumably because of stress – from a job that 74% of the people do not even like or enjoy.

2. Chest Pain: This is the most common presenting symptom of a heart attack. It is described as heavy, crushing, squeezing or stabbing, and is typically located in the mid-chest in the mid-to-lower sternum; it may radiate to the left jaw or the left upper extremity; sometimes it radiates to the back. It may be accompanied by cold, clammy perspiration, nausea, weakness or shortness of breath.

3. Silent: A number of patients suffer from a heart attack without symptoms. Often, this is discovered accidentally, usually through a routine electrocardiogram with findings of old myocardial infarct.

4. Miscellaneous presentation: Patients may develop sudden loss of consciousness, confusion, severe sweating, irregular heart beats, profound weakness or low blood pressure, with or without chest pain.

5. Physical signs: On observation, patients are usually very anxious, fearful, restless, pale, cold and clammy, and at times, hard of breathing. Or, in worst cases, they may be unconscious without pulse or blood pressure. There may be absence of breathing. In some cases, they may be having a seizure of some kind.

Upon physical examination by the medical doctor, there may be many other significant findings that may not be evident to a non-doctor. Some of these may be a murmur from the heart or rales and wheezing from the lungs.

WHAT ARE THE FACTORS THAT CAN BRING ABOUT A HEART ATTACK?

1. Smoking: Cigarette smoking is the most lethal habit and the most significant, preventable cause of premature death. Smokers have a greater risk of developing chronic disorders in their cardiovascular systems, and in many other different organs, causing a multitude of diseases. Arteriosclerotic cardiovascular disease is the chief contributor to the high incidence of deaths from smoking...heart attacks being the main culprit. The tragedy of this very bad habit is not just confined to the people who smoke; unfortunately, even the innocent people, usually the loved ones who live with smokers, or associates who work with them, receive secondary smoke.

About 60,000 deaths annually have been blamed on second hand smoke (other people's smoke)! Cigarette smoke damages the cells in the arterial walls, leaving them vulnerable to plaque formation.

2. Obesity: This is one of the most common conditions in clinical practice, and one of the most challenging to manage. It is defined as body weight 20% or more above the ideal weight. About 33% of Americans fit

this definition. There are now reports from medical journals that there is an increasing incidence of obesity even among young children or teenagers. The risk that obesity gives to the heart is through coronary artery disease and high blood pressure. However, obesity is not only a risk factor for heart disease, but for a myriad of other serious diseases such as cancer, hypertension, multiple sclerosis, arthritis, diabetes, sleep apnea, etc.

3. High cholesterol: The normal recommended daily cholesterol intake should not be more than 300 mg. Total cholesterol in the blood should be under 200 mg. LDL, or the bad cholesterol, should be maintained at below 100 mg. HDL, the good cholesterol, must be over 35. The good cholesterol is cardio-protective meaning that its function is to protect the heart from the devastation from the oxidation of cholesterol and the formation of plaques on the coronary arteries. When a heart attack develops in spite of a normal bad cholesterol or LDL level, the culprit is usually the reduction of the good cholesterol, HDL, to a below-normal range. This is not an infrequent occurrence in medical practice.

4. Stress: "It's not what you eat, it's what's eating you." Stress is brought about by a multitude of factors, from a reckless driver to an obnoxious boss at work. During emergencies, the so-called "fight or flight"

phenomenon is good as it prepares you t
deal with your situation. Whether you fight or
flee, there will be an increase in your heart
rate, tightening of your muscles, constriction
of your vessels so you do not bleed much in
case you get injured or cut. These develop-
ments are brought about by the increased
blood levels of norepinephrine and cortisol.
These chemicals are good for an emergency,
but when they are elevated for long periods of
time they become destructive to the cells of
the body, causing severe damage or even
death. Thus, they are also known as the
death hormones. Approximately 65-80% of
diseases are either directly or indirectly
related to these death hormones.

5. High homocysteine level: Homocysteine is a sulfur-containing amino acid
intermediate that is formed during the
metabolism of methionine, an essential
amino acid derived from dietary protein
(Hospital Practice p. 81, June 15/97). There
is evidence that homocysteine causes injury
to the cells of the inner lining of arteries,
predisposing to platelet adhesion, activation,
and subsequent thrombus formation. It also
reacts with LDL, the combination of which is
taken up by macrophages and subsequently
incorporated into foam cells in early
atherosclerotic plaque.

In the *Preventive Medicine Digest*, volume
4, number 6, Dr. Helme Silvet says that "the
consumption of animal protein raises

homocysteine levels, as the amino acid is a result of the metabolism of this type of protein. A recent Norwegian study also found a direct link between the intake of coffee and homocysteine. The more coffee study participants drank, the higher were the homocysteine levels. Those who were both smokers and heavy coffee drinkers had particularly high levels."

6. Sedentary lifestyle: This is one of the correctable factors that can help prevent the occurrence of a heart attack and premature death. Change this bad habit by engaging in more physical activity like brisk walking, gardening and dancing. Strenuous exercises have to be avoided for they can be detrimental to health as well. Watching TV should be stopped completely or reduced to a minimum – it does not benefit you; in fact, it frequently plants negative seeds into your subconscious, making a person more prone to failure than to success, either in health or in life in general.

7. High fat diet: High fat diet is the second most lethal habit known to man. It is responsible for about 300,000 deaths a year with the usual consequence being heart disease. Cancer is the second major consequence of saturated fats. There is now evidence that shows that a high fat diet is also a risk factor for multiple sclerosis.

The main villain is saturated fat which comes from meats. There is an emerging contention that another form of fat could be more dangerous than saturated fat - it is called transfat and is used in preserved foods such as cakes, cookies and other prepared shelved foods. It is also produced by frying low-quality vegetable oils.

8. High blood pressure: Hypertension is a major risk factor for heart disease and stroke.

This is the most common of all the cardiovascular risk factors, and a major accelerator of plaque formation or atherogenesis. Although there are a number of known causes of hypertension, most doctors label them as "essential", a non-threatening terminology that means "the cause is unknown." In the practice of Medicine, when there is no known etiology, doctors are forced to treat the condition symptomatically only, or even empirically which in the short term maybe beneficial but not in the long term.

THE DIFFERENT STAGES IN THE FORMATION OF PLAQUES (hardening of the arteries):

This list of stages is found in many different medical journals, but the following was adopted from a lecture given at the ACAM meeting in Orlando, Florida in April 1999 by Dr. Soly of Massachusetts:

1. Injury to the inner lining (endothelium) of the blood vessels usually caused by homocysteine.

2. Accumulation of monocytes and macrophages.

3. Aggregation of platelets.

4. Influx of T lymphocytes.

5. Influx of other inflammatory cells.

6. Oxidation of bad cholesterol or LDL.

7. Uptake of oxidized LDL by macrophages in the walls of the vessels producing bloated cells known as foam cells.

8. Increased activity of the smooth muscles.

9. Deposition of collagen, elastin and other tissues.

10. Increased vascularization.

11. Degeneration and weakening of the vessel walls.

12. Calcifications ensue, initially hidden, then may become visible, narrowing the lumen as it progresses.

COULD ATHEROSCLEROSIS BE AN INFECTIOUS DISEASE?

The modifiable risk factors of arteriosclerosis and heart attack have been well known in the medical community. However, there is an emerging, worrisome, seemingly unrelated factor that suggests there may be an infectious element to a heart attack.

According to *Hospital Practice*, volume 34, number 9, September 1999, based on seroepidemiologic investigations, microscopic examination of the atherosclerotic plaques, and animal and human studies have suggested a possible link between Cytomegalovirus, Helicobacter pylori, Chlamydia pneumoniae and the development of atheroscleosis.

TESTS AVAILABLE TO DISCOVER OTHER RISK FACTORS NOT NORMALLY SEEN CLINICALLY (Health Magazine- November 1997)

1. Cholesterol: For many years, people were programmed to watch out for this element because of its relationship with heart attacks, especially with increased levels of total cholesterol and LDL, the bad cholesterol. In the recent past, however, studies have shown that heart attacks develop even in people with normal levels of these two substances, but especially

when the HDL or good cholesterol is below the level of 35.

2. Homocysteine: This amino acid, a by-product of methionine metabolism, is normally found in blood and tissues. When excessive in amounts, it causes injury to the endothelium of arteries, provoking plaque formation.

3. Lipoprotein(a): Lipoproteins are molecules that transport fat throughout the entire body. Lipoprotein(a) is a close relative of the LDL, the bad cholesterol or low-density lipoprotein; both have been linked to causing or accelerating the formation of plaques in arteries.

4. Fibrinogen: This is the substance that holds together the platelets in blood clots. Studies have shown that high levels of fibrinogen increase the incidence of plaque formation. Obesity and smoking can aggravate fibrinogen activity.

5. C-Reactive Protein: This is a non-specific substance that is seen in different conditions. It has been estimated that patients with chest pains with large amounts of this protein in the blood have a greater chance of a heart attack. In a Harvard study conducted years ago, it was postulated that men with high levels of C-reactive protein are three times more likely

to suffer a heart attack and twice as likely to have a stroke!

6. Infection: It has been postulated that heart attacks may be due to infection, especially with the finding of Chlamydia pneumoniae in plaques. If this is confirmed by future studies, we may be categorizing heart attacks as an infectious disease which may be contagious.

IS HEART DISEASE FOUND ONLY IN ADULTS?

Most heart attacks affect adults, not youth, but that is not a contraindication to its development. In fact, in a study done in the Southwest of teenagers aged 16-19 who died resulting from car accidents, it was observed that 100% of those studied already had arteriosclerosis of the aorta (the largest artery in the body), and 50% of the right coronary artery.

In an article published in the December 1999 issue of the *Medical Tribune*, volume 40, number 21, entitled "Heart Disease Starts Early In Life," it was pronounced that heart disease starts developing as early as adolescence, even though symptoms are often undetected until middle age or even later.

In a study of 181 heart transplants 2-6 weeks after transplantation, researchers discovered marked signs of atherosclerosis (hardening) of the coronaries of the donor hearts which were from donors representing all age groups. They found that 26 of 36 donors between the ages of 41 and 50 showed signs of atherosclerosis. The shocking discovery was 1 in 6 teenagers and 1 of 3 people in their twenties were similarly affected.

WHAT TO DO TO
CONFRONT HEART DISEASE

There are a variety of procedures available to health care practitioners, both in orthodox medicine and in complementary medicine, to treat heart disease. Traditional medicine practices treating the symptoms while complementary medicine believes in addressing the root cause of a disease. When we start talking of anti-aging and longevity it is best to discuss this with a health practitioner who believes in both. Heart disease, specifically coronary artery disease, is preventable and when already present, is reversible. Many studies have confirmed this.

In traditional medicine, there are three main modes of management available:

1.   Prescription medicines: While there are occasions where prescription medications are helpful, many of them can have serious side effects and may even be fatal.

2.   Angioplasty: This is an invasive procedure done by inserting a catheter into

the blood vessel of the arm or groin, pushing it to the opening of the coronary artery through the clogged area and inflating a balloon in the hope of dilating or opening up the stenosis or obstruction. It sounds good theoretically, but in reality it is fraught with complications and uncertain results.

More often than not, heart attack becomes a complication, the very reason the procedure is supposed to prevent. Moreover, patients may have to undergo this procedure several times, and with each attempt, complications of a heart attack, stroke, bleeding or sudden death loom large.

According to the *Journal of the American Medical Association*, over 40% of patients are in the same condition within six months after angioplasty! Additionally, an angiogram is done before any therapeutic procedure is done, but according to this same prestigious medical journal, "only about 4% of the patients given angiographs really needed them."

3.   Coronary by-pass surgery: Unless the stenosis involves the left main coronary artery or proximal left anterior descending artery, this surgery should be kept in the museum. But even in these two areas, unless the clogging is more than 90%, other procedures may be even better.

First, the area that is being corrected is very small, maybe amounting to an inch or two.

Second, hardening of the arteries involves the whole 65,000 miles of arteries we have so that by-passing a small segment does not address the total problem.

Third, the death rate during surgery is 1-20%, with the average around 5%. That is 5 people dying out of a 100, and that is 5 people too many.

Fourth, the incidence of repeat surgeries is significant. The tragedy is that after the 3rd or 4th surgery, another by-pass may not be possible anymore because all the usable, superficial veins may have been used up by this time. This is the time when your cardiologist or cardiac surgeon comes to you and declares, "I'm sorry, we cannot do anything more for you. Go home and settle your finances because you can die at anytime."

OTHER OPTIONS

Outside of mainstream medicine there are multitude of options. Although the resistance has lessened over the years, there is still an attitude of some indifference concerning alternative means of therapy.

Generally, I would suggest you explore some other options before considering expensive and sometimes fatal surgery.

The truth is complementary or alternative medicine can offer many choices to heart patients. A multitude of patients all over the world have been helped through alternative means of medical practice. Patients usually seek alternative therapy in secret without telling their primary physician because:

(1) They do not want to hurt the feelings of their doctor,

(2) Some doctors are not receptive to alternative treatments, so the patient is afraid of alienating their doctor, and

(3) Many do not tell because they simply do not consider it important whether their doctor agrees with their alternative choices.

In 1993, Americans spent about $12 billion on alternative modes of treatment. In 1997, this figure leap-frogged to $28 billion. More and more people are seeking the complementary or alternative type of medicine because of the frustrations and costs associated with traditional medicine.

The consensus is that traditional medical care frequently only treats symptoms with no attempt to address the root cause of the disease.

In complementary medicine, the focus is to prevent disease, and when already present, to reverse it. 6 out of 10 Americans are involved in this new paradigm in Medicine.

Coincidentally, there has been an increase in the number of Americans who are 100 years of age or older. In 1960, there were only 3,222 Americans who were 100 years old or over, but in 1997 there were over 100,000. Many believe this is because more people are more health conscious, practicing what they feel will increase their chances of enjoying longevity.

The normal mode of operation in treatment through an alternative physician involves establishing a change in lifestyle, a good diet program, preventing or controlling stress, routine exercise, plus a daily intake of vitamins and antioxidants.

WHY ARE DOCTORS NOT PRESCRIBING VITAMINS, MINERALS AND OTHER ANTI-OXIDANTS?

There are many possible reasons why, but we can perhaps put them in 4 categories:

1.   They do not believe in them.

2.   They do not think they are important.

3.   They do not know anything about them.

4.   Any combination of the above.

One can usually detect the reason when you talk to them during your office visit. I suggest you determine the reason yourself from your own doctor.

Whatever your particular doctor believes, research has clearly demonstrated that antioxidants are extremely beneficial to our health and body.

HOW TO KEEP YOUR HEART HEALTHY AND HAVE A FIGHTING CHANCE TO LIVE A HEALTHY, LONG AND HAPPY LIFE:

1. DIET: I recommend the 60-20-20 formula – 60 grams of carbohydrates, 20 grams of proteins and 20 grams of fat. The saturated fat intake should not exceed 10% of the total calorie intake. The Bible is brimming with teachings and commandments to help keep us healthy. However, due to ignorance and lack of knowledge, we succumb to the destructive temptations and eventually to disease. As one egregious example of disobedience, wittingly or unwittingly, Leviticus 3:17 says,

"It shall be a perpetual statute throughout your generations in all your dwellings: you shall eat neither fat nor blood."

Yet, we continually violate this scripture whenever we eat hamburgers, hot dogs and many other similar food items. These are very tasteful items but they contain both blood and fats. The Lord did not explain why He prohibits us from eating these kinds of food, but medical science now points out that there is much cholesterol, saturated fats and even homocysteine that are detrimental to our cardiovascular system that can eventually develop into a heart attack or a stroke.

In Isaiah 55:2, it says, *"...listen carefully to Me, and eat what is good...."* The word "good" here does not refer to taste but rather to what is healthy.

If good health and longevity are what we are after, then some of the foods we should eat are found in Genesis 1:29 which says,

"And God said, See, I have given you every herb that yields seed which is on the face of all the earth, and every tree whose fruits yield seed; to you it shall be food."

After the great flood in Genesis 9:3, God modified our diet and added meat as food. The lists of what we can and cannot eat are found in Leviticus 11 and Deuteronomy 14. The diet factor is just one of many important factors in the prevention of a cardiovascular catastrophe.

2. EXERCISE: There is <u>overwhelming</u> scientific evidence that regular physical

activity produces a wide range of physical and mental health benefits, including a sound and healthy heart. Exercise as simple as walking or gardening strengthens the heart and cardiovascular system, increases energy and enhances the state of mind.

Exercise can stop osteoporosis, lower cholesterol and blood pressure, and decrease heart disease and certain cancers. In an article published in the *Emergency Medicine* June 1998, a 12-year study showed that brisk walking of about two miles "appears to protect older men not only against coronary heart disease but also against cancer."

3. STRESS MANAGEMENT: Removing the offending factor is the best measure to deal with stress. Other measures such as prayer and meditation on the scriptures will give you peace that is beyond compre-hension. Exercise will also help in managing stress because of the secretions of neuro-transmitters, especially endorphins, which give a feeling of wellbeing.

4. ATTITUDE: People with positive attitudes do not get sick as often as those with negative attitudes, and when they do get sick, they get better faster.

5. ANTIOXIDANTS: It has been said that the crux of coronary artery disease is the oxidation of the bad cholesterol, LDL, by free

radicals or oxidants. It goes without saying that the antidote to these is the antioxidants.

The 4 basic antioxidants useful for general health are Vitamin C, Vitamin E, Beta Carotene and Selenium. However, there are other natural products that are used against heart challenges like Coenzyme Q 10, quercetin, pycnogenol, folic acid, Vitamin B6, Vitamin B12, alpha lipoic acid, French paradox, calcium, magnesium, etc. The product of choice is CardioLife.

6. CHELATION THERAPY: This is an option available to all heart and stroke sufferers and those with circulation problems. This therapy is less invasive and less dangerous compared to coronary by-pass surgery and angioplasty. Chelation therapy is a painless procedure to remove toxic materials from the body, especially the cardiovascular system, to improve circulation and reverse disease. This procedure is performed in the medical office, and takes about 1 ½ to 3 hours depending on the physician.

REASONS FOR TAKING VITAMINS, SUPPLE-MENTS, ETC. (Applied Biometrics)

   a.   62% - prevents disease

   b.   54% - increases energy

   c.   40% - improves fitness

d.   31% - increases alertness

e.   27% - reduces stress

f.   25% - treats medical problems

g.   21% - fights depression

CHAPTER TWO

---

2 CAUSE OF DEATH – CANCER

"There is a way that seems right to a man, but its end is the way of death" Proverb 16:25

The development of cancer is purely from our habits and environment which we may think as inconsequential, but they are destructive to our body. These bad habits are so ubiquitous that they blend with some of our good habits and are embraced as part and parcel of our modern society.

For example, young teenagers are learning to smoke at a very early age because they think it is socially hip, and it makes them look more mature or professional. Eating high amounts of saturated fat, especially from fast food eateries, is a cultural fad because the food tastes good and is quick. Or staying under the sun to get a deep tan to impress others. All of these activities are detrimental to the body cells that predispose us to developing cancer. These all blatantly disregard good health practices. But we think it is the way to go because that is what "everybody else is doing."

In the discussion of the molecular outlaws attacking normal cells in the body, when the nucleus is the one targeted, two conditions are bound to develop, namely, premature aging and cancer. These conditions are both preventable and reversible. But we must seek knowledge and understanding so we can develop a lifestyle that will give us good health and a long life.

According to the American Cancer Society, the sad truth is clearly evident in the war against cancer that was initiated by President Nixon in 1972. The study shows that over $28 billion has been spent to combat this dreaded disease but it continues its menacing journey, already killing over 10 million people. Additionally, there are about 1.3 million new cases of cancer that develop every year.

Among the factors that predispose us to cancer are:

1. Smoking

2. Obesity

3. Saturated fat

4. Ultraviolet rays

5. X-ray radiation

6. Age

7. Stress

8. Passive smoking

9. Low consumption of fruits and vegetables

10. Exposure to heavy metals such as Cadmium, etc.

11. Chronic diseases such as COPD, cirrhosis, etc.

12. HIV

According to *CA* – a Cancer Journal for Clinicians, Jan/Feb.1998, the following are the 10 leading sites by sex of the estimated new cancer cases:

Male

1. Prostate---------------------------------29%

2. Lung and Bronchus---------------------15%

3. Colon and Rectum----------------------10%

4. Urinary Bladder--------------------------6%

5. Non-Hodgkin's Lymphoma--------------5%

6. Skin Melanoma---------------------------4%

7. Kidney and Renal Pelvis---------------- 3%

8. Leukemia---------------------------------3%

9. Oral Cavity and Pharynx----------------3%

10. Stomach----------------------------------2%

11. Others---------------------------------20%

Female

1.   Breast------------------------------30%

2.   Lung and Bronchus---------------13%

3.   Colon and Rectum-----------------11%

4.   Endometrium-----------------------6%

5.   Ovary--------------------------------4%

6.   Non-Hodgkin's Lymphoma---------4%

7.   Melanoma----------------------------3%

8.   Cervix--------------------------------2%

9.   Pancreas-----------------------------2%

10. Urinary Bladder----------------------2%

11. Others--------------------------------23%

LEADING CANCER DEATHS
ACCORDING TO SITES

Male

1.   Lung and Bronchus ---------------32%

2.   Prostate ----------------------------13%

3. Colon and Rectum------------------9%

4. Pancreas --------------------------5%

5. Leukemia --------------------------4%

6. Non-Hodgkin's Lymphoma--------4%

7. Esophagus--------------------------3%

8. Liver and Intrahepatic bile duct---3%

9. Stomach----------------------------3%

10. Urinary Bladder--------------------3%

11. Others-----------------------------21%

Female

1. Lung and Bronchus ---------------25%

2. Breast------------------------------16%

3. Colon and Rectum----------------11%

4. Pancreas---------------------------6%

5. Ovary-------------------------------5%

6. Leukemia---------------------------4%

7. Non-Hodgkin's Lymphoma--------4%

8. CNS---------------------------------2%

9. Endometrium ---------------------2%

10. Stomach----------------------------2%

11. Others-------------------------------23%

Neoplastic disease, or cancer, is a very important public health concern all over the world. In 1998, it was estimated that in the United States there were approximately 1 million cases of basal cell and squamous cell skin carcinoma, 36,900 cases of breast carcinoma in situ, 21,100 cases of melanoma carcinoma in situ and 1,228,600 new cases of other invasive cancers.

As stated above, the top three cancers in men are cancers of the prostate, lung and bronchus, and colon and rectum. Prostate is the leading cancer site, accounting for 29% of new cancer cases.

Among women, the top three cancers are that of the breast, lung and bronchus, and colon and rectum. These three account for more than 50% of new cancer cases in women. Breast cancer alone accounts for more than 30% of all cancers in women, numbering approximately 178,700 new cases in 1998.

CANCER DEATHS

Cancer is the second most common cause of death in America accounting for approximately 564,800 deaths in 1998 – that is about 1,500 people a day, or approximately one death every second.

EUROPEAN CONSENSUS STATEMENT ON LUNG CANCER: RISK FACTORS AND PREVENTION – published in the *CA* – Cancer Journal for Clinicians volume 48, number 3, May/June 1998, pp 167-175.

The article was based on the Hohenheim Consensus Meeting organized by the WHO Europe and the German Ministry of Health.

There is consistent evidence that consumption of fruits and vegetables is associated with lower incidence of cancer in general and of the lungs in particular. It is presumed that the multiple components of these foods act in concert to produce the overall beneficial effect.

There is evidence that consumption of Beta Carotene with increased plasma levels show low incidence of cancer. There is experimental evidence, based on animal studies and cell culture, etc., that dietary components like antioxidants, minerals and trace elements interfere with the growth and progression of lung cancer.

From both the in vitro and in vivo studies, there is evidence that lycopene, lutein, beta carotene, Vitamin A, Vitamin E and Vitamin C and some trace elements interfere with lung cancer growth. Beta Carotene, Vitamins C and E are important compounds that protect the lungs from oxidation.

MALIGNANT MELANOMA

This is the most invasive and deadly cancer involving the skin. This is usually attributed to excessive exposure to ultraviolet rays, especially between the hours of 10 a.m. and 4 p.m.

This is the most common cancer in women ages 25-29 and number 2 for women ages 30-34. The incidence of this cancer has increased from 1 in 1500 ten years ago to 1 in 75 today.

There are approximately 44,000 new cases of melanoma every year with about 10,000 deaths. 79% of all skin cancer deaths are from melanoma.

PERCENTAGES OF CANCER DEATHS ATTRIBUTED TO VARIOUS FACTORS

1. Diet – 35%

2. Tobacco – 30%

3. Occupation – 4%

4. Radon – 2-3%

5. Pollution – 2%

6. Medical x-rays – 0.5%

7. Ultraviolet rays and others – 25%

Approximately 800,000 new cancers are diagnosed every year. It is believed that at least 80% of all cancers can be prevented just with a change in lifestyle, including the increased intake of antioxidants.

People perish for lack of knowledge.

TRADITIONAL TREATMENTS:

1.   Surgery: This is usually done when the cancer is still localized and has not spread to distant organs or sites. Once metastasis has set in, surgery may only be indicated to alleviate an emergency situation such as intestinal bleeding or urinary tract obstruction (but this is not done as curative measure).

2.   Radiation: Like surgery, this is done in certain forms of cancer and also when the cancer is confined to a local area. There are occasions when this is prescribed along with surgery and/or chemotherapy. The main problem with this mode of treatment is it works by killing the cancer cells, but during the process normal cells are also killed so that the patient ends up with a severely weakened immune system which often produces unbearable side effects.

3.   Chemotherapy: The rationale for the use of chemotherapy is to annihilate the immune system with the hope that it will regenerate and become more powerful to

combat the neoplastic process. However, good theories do not always manifest as good realities. In fact, more cancer patients die from the effects of chemotherapy than from cancer itself. And yet we continue to subject patients to this torture rather than offer them the less glamorous but seemingly more predictable and effective alternative way of treatment.

ALTERNATIVE TREATMENT

Complementary or alternative medicine is coming to the forefront because of growing disenchantment with some of the orthodox ways of medicine. The changing personality of traditional medicine, with the increasing power of managed care, sometimes makes patients feel more like numbers instead of people. In the interest of time, much of the communication between the doctor and the patients has been greatly reduced. There is also increasing awareness of patients that traditional medicine focuses primarily on treating symptoms instead of the disease. These factors encourage people to seek out additional health care systems that address the root cause of the disease in the hope of reversing it.

In the June 10, 1999 issue of the *Medical Tribune*, it disclosed the first-ever symposium on alternative and complementary medicine hosted by the American College of Clinical Oncology and the American Cancer Society. It was agreed that physicians need to learn more about medical cares that are not standard or traditional. They noted that alternative medicine is a rapidly growing business. Dr. Davis Rosenthal, a professor of medicine at Harvard University, pointed out that in 1997, an estimated 42 % of Americans used some form of complementary or alternative medicine. He added that alternative medicine had 629 million patient visits compared to 386 million office visits to traditional doctors.

In an interview with *Medical Tribune*, Dr. Vint of San Diego indicated that there is much evidence about the effectiveness of various nutrients in preventing cancer. The problem is that even when the evidence is published in mainstream journals, physicians often are slow to adopt, or even ignore the findings. He noted as an example the Physicians Health Study by Gann et al in *Cancer Research* (1999) that demonstrated a strong inverse relationship between lycopene levels and both the presence of prostate cancer and tumor aggressiveness.

In short, the only hope for cancer to be prevented or reversed is through the understanding that the medical doctor is not the sole person responsible for treatment, but that the patient must also take responsibility. That involves being willing to wade through massive and often confusing or contradictory information available. The individual person must decide what needs to be done and must not rely completely on the doctors who are mostly busy treating cancer rather than preventing or reversing it.

Tragically, many mainline doctors do not share what the practitioners of alternative medicine believe...that most diseases can be prevented and reversed.

WHAT CAN ONE DO TO LESSEN THE POSSIBILITY OF DEVELOPING CANCER?

1. Stop Smoking: This is the most important, preventable factor in chronic diseases including cancer. According to the National Cancer Institute, there are more than 4,000 chemicals in tobacco and tobacco smoke. Sixty (60) of these compounds are carcinogenic (cancer-producing) such as tar, formaldehyde, benzene, cyanide, carbon monoxide, phenols, ammonia, nitrosamine, nicotine and others. It will take 5 years after stopping smoking before the incidence of cancer of the lung, mouth, throat and esophagus is reduced to half that of a pack-a-day smoker. After 10 years of being smoke-free, the risk of lung cancer is the same as a non-smoker. At this point all pre-cancerous cells have been replaced.

2. Obesity: This is the second most important factor in the development of cancer. Statistics show that obesity increases the incidence cancer of the female reproductive organs, namely, uterus and ovaries 5-fold, the gall bladder 3-fold,

prostate 2-fold and double that of the breast and colon.

3. Ultraviolet rays: Exposure to the sun, especially between 10 a.m. and 4 p.m., for more than 30 minutes will increase the incidence of skin cancer. This is attributed to the formation of free radicals attacking normal skin cells. There are various forms of skin cancer, like basal cell carcinoma, but the most deadly is malignant melanoma which has shown significant increase in the last few years. Avoid exposure to the sun as much as possible for over half an hour.

4. Eat plenty of fruits and vegetables: They contain cancer-fighting ingredients like vitamins, fiber and roughage. 5 to 8 servings are recommended. In a study of more than 2,000 Welch men, those who ate the most fruit had half the incidence of cancer death. Lycopene, a powerful antioxidant abundant in tomato products, is a powerful fighter against cancer of the prostate. In a study of 48,000 men at Harvard, those who took significant amounts of lycopene had a 21 % lower incidence of prostate cancer; those who had 2-4 servings of tomato sauce a week had a 34% lower risk. Even those who consumed 2-4 servings of pizza a week reduced the risk by 15%. The caveat in pizzas, however, is not to over-indulge in cheeses and meats.

Onions, best regarded as antibacterial, contain a compound with anti-cancer properties called "allylic sulfides". A four-year study of 3,123 individuals in the Netherlands showed that those who consumed at least half an onion daily had half the risk of stomach cancer.

In a study of people who ate a significant amount of cabbage, broccoli, Brussels sprouts, mustard greens, kale and cauliflower (the group is called "Brassicas"), there was 40% reduction in risk. These vegetables contain sulforaphane, an anti-cancer compound (perhaps the most powerful of all) which appears to boost natural defenses and lowers cancer risk by blocking enzymes that draw carcinogens into healthy cells.

Soy products contain phytoestrogens which may fight off prostate cancer. The chemical that fights cancer is genistein which blocks the formation of new blood vessels around new tumors, stopping their growth. The incidence of prostate cancer in Japan is 35% lower than that in America, presumably because the Japanese consume about 20-80 mg. of genistein daily compared to Americans who only consume 1-3 milligrams.

One good use of soy is soy milk in cereals. Canadian researchers reviewed 13 studies involving more than 15,000 people and found that those who ate the most fiber had half the risk of colorectal cancer. They also found that an additional 13 grams of fiber a day could reduce colorectal cancer risk by 31 %.

Eating all forms of vegetables is also recommended in the prevention of cancer. For example, grapes have a substance, resveratrol, that attacks cancer at several stages, and even reverses it according to John Pezzuto, director of the collaborative research program at the University of Illinois College of Pharmacy (from *Men's Health,* May 1997).

5.   Drink 4-8 glasses of water. The most ideal water to drink is distilled or rain water. However, because our atmosphere is now so polluted, rain water may not be your first choice. In a study at the University of Washington of 462 men, it was discovered that those who drank at least 4 glasses of water daily had a 32 % lower risk of colon cancer (ditto).

6.   Stress: It has been postulated that stress can cause lowering of the immune system, making one vulnerable to all kinds of medical challenges including cancer. In a study at the University of Pennsylvania, mice were injected with tumor cells and then subjected to electric shocks. These mice were divided into two groups: one was allowed to escape the shocks and the other was not. The group that received the shocks developed tumors at a faster rate. This probably follows the rationale behind the attitude of a patient.

Those with good attitudes seem to survive their challenges more than those with a negative attitude (*Men's Health*).

7.   Avoid diagnostic x-rays if at all possible.

8.   Avoid exposure to heavy metals.

9.   Avoid pollution.

10. Avoid HIV infection and AIDS – cancers known as sarcomas are prevalent in AIDS patients.

11. Antioxidants and NK Power, a product specifically used to increase the activity of the Natural Killer (NK) cells to kill bacteria and cancer cells.

CHAPTER THREE

3 CAUSE OF DEATH – STROKE

A centurion in Capernaum said, "Lord, my servant is lying at home paralyzed, dreadfully tormented." And Jesus said to him, "I will come and heal him" Matthew 8:5-7.

Stroke or cerebrovascular accident (CVA) is the number three cause of death in America. It essentially has the same pathophysiology as a heart attack which is arteriosclerosis. When these two diseases are put together, they comprise 53% of all deaths every year!

There are approximately 500,000 strokes every year causing an annual mortality of about 200,000 which is equivalent to one death every 22 minutes. Stroke is the major cause of serious long-term disability. Although stroke is classified as a disease of the elderly, it can and does affect even younger people. In fact, about 1,000 teenagers develop a stroke annually.

There are 3 forms of CVA or stroke namely, thrombosis, embolism and hemorrhage. The most common is thrombosis causing ischemia; it comprises at least 75% of all strokes, about

15% for cerebral embolism and another 10% for intracranial hemorrhage or bleeding.

Cerebral thrombosis is due to arteriosclerosis causing diminished blood flow to the brain. This could start as a TIA or transient ischemic attack which means a temporary occurrence of reversible symptoms of a stroke. Cerebral embolism is usually due to some heart problem with thrombotic material forming in the left side of the heart which could either be the left atrium or left ventricle, and from the mitral valves. Although embolism can be thrown to any of the peripheral circulation, the most serious is when it involves the brain, causing a stroke.

Cerebral hemorrhage is the most dangerous of these three and the most difficult to manage. This could happen spontaneously, especially in people with hypetension but it can be due to a ruptured aneurysm, ruptured arteriovenous malformation, trauma, bleeding from brain tumors or anticoagulation and from cocaine and ampethamines.

WHAT ARE THE CLINICAL SYMPTOMS?

According to a survey by the Awareness and Knowledge of Stroke Prevention group in 1996, and reported by the National Stroke Association and the Gallup organization, the following were the symptoms:

58% - weakness/numbness/paralysis of face and extremities

32% - speech difficulty

15% - dizziness/loss of balance

12% - headaches

9% - loss or blurring of vision

4% - pass out or black out

17% - unknown

PATHOPHYSIOLOGY OF STROKE AS REPORTED BY DR. STARKMAN IN THE EMERGENCY MEDICINE SUPPLEMENT OCT. 1997

There is a 6-hour window in which a stroke patient can be treated effectively, and prevent complete brain damage. This window can be larger or smaller in individual patients. Nevertheless, time is very crucial because the longer the treatment is withheld there is a danger of increasing irreversible brain damage.

During a stroke, the neurons at the core of the area of the brain that is deprived of its normal blood supply will die unless blood circulation is restored within the time frame allotted. Depending on the area of the brain affected, signs and symptoms may manifest.

RISK FACTORS FOR STROKE (Dr. Ralph Sacco – Seminar, Nov. 1997)

Ischemic stroke is a major public health concern because it is more disabling than fatal, and results in tremendous financial drain from the medical treatment which can be exhaustive and prolonged and loss of productivity. Identifying the risk factors and doing something about them is the cornerstone in the prevention of this catastrophic malady. The three major factors are:

1.   Hypertension

2.   Smoking cigarettes

3.   Increased cholesterol and triglycerides

HYPERTENSION: Except for old age, high blood pressure is at the forefront of all the risk factors. There is a direct relationship between the risk of stroke and increasing blood pressure, either systolic or diastolic. There is a high degree of prevalence of high blood pressure in both men and women, and this prevalence increases with age. Reduction in blood pressure, even slightly, could translate into a substantial reduction in stroke incidence.

It is estimated that 246,500 strokes could be prevented from the control of hypertension alone, and could result in a savings of $12.33 billion!

CIGARETTE SMOKING: This is a major public health problem causing 410,000 deaths each year. Smoking has been established as a significant risk factor, although the mechanism is unknown. However, it has been postulated to be due the acceleration of atherosclerosis. It is closely associated with plaque formation of the carotid artery. Other areas concerning the damage that smoking could do include increased blood viscosity, enhanced platelet aggregation, elevation of blood pressure and increased coagulation and elevated fibrinogen.

Stroke risk was increased twofold in people who smoke more than 40 cigarettes a day compared to those who smoke less than 10 cigarettes a day. It has been estimated that 61,000 strokes could be prevented from the control of cigarette smoking with an associated savings of $3 billion per year.

INCREASED CHOLESTEROL AND TRI-GLYCERIDES: These are more closely related to coronary artery disease; nevertheless, they are also risk factors in strokes.

Another risk factor that has recently identified is increased lipoprotein(a) levels. Improvement in the level of these different factors will translate into savings of lives, disability and costs.

THE TREATMENTS

The traditional treatments for stroke include:

1.   Surgery: Mainly carotid endarter-ectomy. About 110,000 procedures are done per year, and half of them are for patients without symptoms.

2.   Anticoagulation: Using a blood thinner like Coumadin and aspirin

3.   Prescription medications such as dipyridamole and ticlopidine and clopidogrel.

4.   For acute cases: Thrombolytic therapy, using sterptokinase and tissue plasminogen activator.

As one can tell, the traditional management of patients with a stroke is directed mostly in stabilizing the acute phase while in chronic cases, it is doing physical or speech therapy as the case may be. There is no attempt to reverse the root cause of the disease, which is usually due to arteriosclerosis.

However, these patients may benefit more from the use of alternative therapy. Among the treatments by alternative practitioners...all the different factors mentioned under Chapter One for heart attacks are applicable here. To review, here are some things that we need to do:

1.   Complete change of lifestyle.

2.   Remove the factors contributing to the disease process such as high cholesterol, smoking, obesity, high blood pressure.

3. Change the diet: start with vegetarian foods.

4. Stress management: Stress Away capsules, a natural product to reduce or remove stress is used in this situation. Exercise is also a good antidote for stress.

5. Take plenty of antioxidants and other vitamins, minerals and fatty acids including natural blood thinners. Cardiolife should be the core of this antioxidant therapy.

6. Chelation therapy: This is the best kept secret in Medicine! Tens of thousands have been helped by this procedure all over the world, but it still has not been approved for this purpose by the FDA. The reason? No pharmaceutical company is willing to perform a double-blind study to confirm its efficacy because the chelation patent has long expired.

Spending tons of money, usually between $75 - $500 million, to study a product is not a good business practice if there is no patent to give the manufacturer sole marketing rights for 18 years.

However, there are numerous studies in other countries attesting to its usefulness, but these studies, and the testimonies of countless patients are not good enough to satisfy the requirements of the government. It is, however, legal for any doctor to use chelation therapy any way he determines because it is already approved for removing toxic heavy metals.

CHAPTER FOUR

4 CAUSE OF DEATH – DRUG REACTIONS

"...do you not know that your body is the temple of the Holy Spirit?" 1 Corinthians 6:19

When the government makes a report of the ten most common causes of death every year, death from drug reactions is never mentioned. But year after year people lose their lives because of drugs. In point of fact, this is the number 4 cause of death!

This is the irony of ironies – drugs designed to help people get better become one of the most common causes of death! It is astonishing to think that with the best of intentions, in the best of hands, something so fatal can be so common.

In medical practice, there is an old adage from the days of Hippocrates that says, "First, do no harm." I am certain that most physicians have this in mind when treating patients. They do the best they can, but unfortunately, in the use of prescription drugs, side effects or untoward reactions develop.

More than 2 million people have drug reactions; 1.5 million are hospitalized, and over

136,000 die every year taking drugs manufactured by legitimate pharmaceutical companies, prescribed by licensed medical doctors, and approved by the ever-so-powerful FDA.

And these do not include the 7,000 deaths due to errors in administering the medications!

The National Academy of Sciences reported in December, 1999 that medical errors in hospitals cause up to 98,000 deaths every year.

For unknown reasons, in the usual list of the top ten causes of death, drug reactions are not listed as a cause of death. We cannot really draw any conclusion from this exclusion, although it is common knowledge that drug companies are a very powerful group, and to list their products as a cause of death could be harmful to the drug industry.

Dr. Larry Doss, in a statement in *The Longevity Report*, volume 10, number 1, says "It's about time that mainstream medicine stopped subjecting patients to the profiteering drug companies and their debilitating drugs." And it is also about time that we considered drug reactions as a disease – "iatrogenic" disease, which means "a disease caused by doctors" that kills hundreds of thousands of innocent people.

We need doctors. They play an important role in helping sick people get better. But if we can help it, we need to indulge in preventive medicine to avoid being at risk and subjected to this 4th cause of death. The saying, "An ounce of prevention is better than a pound of cure" is true, particularly in the area of achieving health. It is far better to do those things necessary to "prevent" a sickness than try and cure the sickness after the body has been abused.

To prevent this terrible cause of death from happening to us, we must do our best to stay in tip-top shape so that we do not need to visit a doctor's office and receive prescription drugs for an illness that could have been avoided in the first place.

Ideally, doctors should be treating diseases rather than just symptoms. As a cardiologist, a typical example of a disease we often see is congestive heart failure (CHF). In CHF, a patient manifests symptoms such as shortness of breath, extreme fatigue, maybe chest pains, unable to sleep flat on his back, more comfortable sitting up, and is pale or even cyanotic. This patient has many findings upon physical examination, from noises in the lungs called "rales", to wheezing with a rapid heart rate, to swelling of the ankles or legs, etc.

When a diagnosis of congestive heart failure is made, the patient is treated, among other things, with complete bed rest, a low-salt diet, oxygen, diuretics, digitalis, a sedative, stool softener and a medication to help the patient sleep. There may be other things the doctor can do, but typically, this is the way CHF is treated.

Once the acute phase is addressed, the doctor then looks for other problems that have caused the CHF such as high blood pressure, high cholesterol and coronary artery disease. The doctor will try his best to do something about these problems.

Let us assume, for example, that the cause of CHF in this particular case is coronary artery disease. Usually there is high cholesterol and high blood pressure associated with this condition, and a plan of treatment is outlined:

1. Treatment of the congestive heart failure – as mentioned previously.

2. Treatment of high blood pressure – usually a patient is put on low salt diet and given drugs to lower the blood pressure, sometimes with just diuretics, but often with other anti-hypertensives.

3. Treatment of high cholesterol – with low cholesterol diet and cholesterol-lowering drugs.

When the patient is better, one of two things will happen: either he is sent home and kept on the listed treatment, or he is told to have a coronary angiogram. Lets venture to say that a coronary by-pass surgery is done. After a period of recovery in the hospital, he is sent home, normally with all the medications he was prescribed before for congestive heart failure, high cholesterol, high blood pressure and the other medications, with instructions to follow up his treatment with periodic visits to the doctor's office to monitor progress.

This is usually the way this problem is treated. The doctor has performed a service, the patient is free of symptoms, and the family is satisfied.

But was the disease treated or was the treatment only for the symptoms?

You might say, "What's the difference?"

A very important one.

If the treatment is just for the symptoms, then the problem is bound to come back. Whereas, if the treatment also addresses the cause of the disease, it probably will not return.

In most cases, the treatment is only for the symptoms. Even by-pass surgery only addresses the symptoms. The basic root problem here is not the occlusion or blockage of the coronary arteries, but the cause of that occlusion – arteriosclerosis, or the hardening of the arteries.

The next question is, "Didn't the by-pass surgery treat the arteriosclerosis?"

No, it did not! It only addressed the area that was by-passed which is usually just one or two inches long. In arteriosclerosis, the entire arterial system of approximately 65,000 miles is involved so that even though there maybe a detour for about two inches, the rest of the arteries are still diseased!

The advantage of complementary, integrated, alternative or preventive medicine is that this practice focuses more on the preventing of the disease from developing. When the disease is already present, then the objective is to reverse it. Traditional medicine normally does not focus on attempting to reverse a disease.

Basically, all prescription drugs, when abused or mis-prescribed, can kill. Instead of discussing all of them here (that would take volumes of books), let us just tackle the example given in the treatment of congestive heart failure, a very common condition in hospitalized patients.

1.   Diuretics – there are numerous types of this drug. These medications can lead to excessive diuresis with water and electrolyte depletion. They can have hypersensitivity reaction, CNS, cardiovascular, hematologic, gastrointestinal or dermatologic reactions.

2.   Digitalis – the mainstay in the treatment of heart failure, can be a killer, too. It kills by producing arrhythmia or irregular heartbeats or heart blocks. It can also

produce dermatologic, gastrointestinal or central nervous system reactions.

3. Antihypertensives – they can have many unpleasant reactions including cardiovascular, central nervous system, gastrointestinal, psychiatric, respiratory, urinary and hematologic. As a disability, impotence is most notably ubiquitous. When a diagnosis of hypertension is made, the doctor usually prescribes a vasodilator to make the circumference of the blood vessels bigger, thus lowering the blood pressure. Consequently, this effect causes the pulse rate to increase, and when this happens, a second drug is prescribed to slow down the heart. Unfortunately, this kind of drug usually causes the retaining of fluid so that a third drug is prescribed, the diuretics. These diuretics do not just remove water - they also remove calcium, magnesium, potassium, B-vitamins, antioxidants. The result? Water and electrolyte imbalance develops with vitamin and mineral deficiencies.

4. Anticholesterol agents – can affect the liver and other gastrointestinal system; can have adverse effect on the cardiovascular, CNS, respiratory, musculoskeletal, dermatologic or hematologic systems.

5. Sedative/hypnotics – can cause nervous system problems such as confusion, depression, double vision, loss of libido and many others, but especially addiction.

Some examples of drugs that were initially approved by the FDA as "safe" but then later withdrawn from the market when dangerous side affects were manifested, include:

a.   Redux – was taken off the market in August, 1997 because it was implicated in heart valve problems. It was in the market for 17 months.

b.   Posicor, a blood pressure medication, was withdrawn in June, 1998 after it was in the market for a year. Posicor caused serious problems when it interacted with numerous other medications.

c.   Duract – an alternative to narcotics for short-term pain relief for pain after surgery. It was in the market for 7 months and was withdrawn because people died and others required liver transplants.

Some examples of other drugs, approved by the FDA as safe, but now having reports of adverse side effects, but not yet withdrawn from the market.

a.   Viagra – the very popular anti-impotence drug. In an article written in the *Sun Sentinel* on June 13, 1999, it was reported that since the approval of Viagra about a year ago, there have been 130 deaths following its use.

b.   Rezulin – approved two years ago, 43 patients with adult-onset diabetes suffered liver failure after taking it, 28 died and 7 others required liver transplants. (Before this book went to press, Rezulin was withdrawn from the market in March, 2000 after being linked to at least 61 deaths from liver poisoning. It was used by about 750,000 Americans.)

DRUG AND SURGICAL RISKS

According to *Sun-Sentinel*, June 13, 1999, approving a drug for clinical use and the monitoring of side effects is fraught with inefficiencies.

The FDA approved 53 drugs in 1996, 39 in 1997 and 30 in 1998 - in contrast to the 1980s when an average of 22 drugs were approved each year. The critics of the FDA drug-approval process, who include prominent doctors, members of Congress and representatives from public interest groups, cite a host of problems ranging from researchers who are subjected to little oversight, to intense pressure within the FDA to approve drugs rapidly.

The panels of experts, called institutional review boards, entrusted to review and approve all research involving humans, is overworked, handling hundreds of proposals, and often take only a cursory look before approving clinical trials. Moreover, they have little time to read annual reports from researchers whose studies are under way.

Board members are resigning from busier panels because they do not have time. Finding replacements is difficult. Those who remain on panels often do not have adequate knowledge about sophisticated new research.

In the last 2 years, five drugs were pulled from the market because of life-threatening problems discovered after approval for sale.

Why?

Because the FDA approves a drug if it deems the benefits to patients outweigh the risks. But there is no specific gauge for this criterion; it is a subjective opinion. A survey in 1998 by the Public Citizen Health Research Group revealed that 19 of 53 agency medical officers who responded to the survey thought 27 new drugs they reviewed in the last 3 years did not warrant approval, but the FDA allowed them on the market anyway.

The *Gero Vita International* newsletter has compiled shocking statistics regarding many myths that have been labeled cures. For example:

• Most of drugs prescribed my doctors do little to correct the underlying condition. In fact, they can even multiply the problems. The prestigious *British Medical Journal*, read by almost all medical doctors, reports that up to 23% of men become impotent because of the medications they consume.

- A powerful "blocker" heart medication actually <u>increases</u> the risk of heart attacks by 60% - according to the American Heart Association.

- Studies by Harvard University and the U.S. government show that <u>85% of all bypass surgeries are not necessary</u>.

According to the TV program 20/20 shown on April 5, 2000, "Going to the hospital is dangerous to your health." Two hundred people die everyday due to medical errors, and the # 1 mistake is wrong medication. In addition, there have been 50,000 surgeries done in the wrong site or part of the body in the last 5 years.

WHAT CAN YOU DO?

How do you prevent these unnecessary errors, side effects and drug interactions?

1. Be knowledgeable about the medicines you are taking.

2. Ask your doctor to explain to you what to anticipate, both good and bad.

3. Ask your doctor if there is another option to consider other than the taking of any prescription drugs.

4. Pray to the Lord for guidance as there are natural products that can be used in practically all medical problems. These

products are usually free of side reactions or
toxicity.

CHAPTER FIVE

5 CAUSE OF DEATH – LUNG DISEASES

"And the Lord God formed man of the dust of the ground, and breathed into his nostrils the breath of life..."
Genesis 2:7

Lung diseases are the number five cause of death. These diseases range from the acute infectious diseases such as pneumonia and bronchitis to the more chronic ones like asthma and emphysema.

According to the American Lung Association, as reported by the *Journal of Longevity*, volume 5, number 12, the death rate from breathing illnesses are rising fast. The incidence of asthma has more than doubled in the last few years. Deaths from emphysema are up by 40%. Air pollution is the major factor in the rise in lung diseases. Our atmosphere is so polluted that with every breath we inhale a dangerous multitude of pollutants such as carbon monoxide, nitrogen dioxide, ozone, sulfur dioxide and particulate matter. Each pollutant carries specific health risks.

Ozone is the major harmful ingredient in smog. Lower atmosphere ozone often becomes dangerously high on hot, sunny days. This has a devastating effect on the lungs. It inflames, causes changes to breathing passages, and decreases the lungs' working ability.

Nitrogen dioxide is produced when fuel is burned in cars and power plants. It can trigger an asthma attack while constricting airways.

Particulate matter consists of microscopic particles from the burning of industrial fuels and the operation of diesel vehicles. These are embedded deep into the lungs where they can cause many diverse medical problems.

KNOW YOUR RESPIRATORY SYSTEM

The respiratory system is one of the most vital systems in our body. Its main organ, the lung, is responsible for the most important element in life – oxygen! A person can sustain life without food for weeks, or without water for days, but lack of oxygen is a killer in just about 4 minutes.

When an emergency happens in the hospital and a "code blue" is announced on the inter-com, a staff of emergency personnel comprised of doctors, nurses, technicians and others rush to the area of emergency immediately. Each knows that the patient has only 4 minutes of time. If circulation and/or breathing is not restored within this short time period, the patient is in danger of being "brain dead." Once brain cells are deprived of oxygen for about 4 minutes, they die and never, ever recover.

The two main diseases that are well known to everyone and that affect the respiratory system are cancer and emphysema, or chronic obstructive lung disease (COPD). However, there are other conditions affecting this organ that are less well known, but nevertheless, can be as fatal and debilitating as the first two. The biggest in this group is the pneumonias which normally are bacterial, viral or fungal. Next is asthma which can be related to infection, allergies, irritation due to inhaled pollutants, stress, strenuous exercise or as a side effect of a prescription drug. Finally, there is tuberculosis, which in the recent past has managed to climb up to prominence because of its close relationship with AIDS.

There are about 10 million new cases of TB worldwide and 3 million of them die every year. In addition, there is a growing incidence of resistant strain tuberculosis which is harder to treat, and more fatal. Everyone must be tested for TB, and if the skin test is positive, a work up for active TB must be done. If there is no evidence of active TB, and the person is under 35 years of age, prophylactic treatment must be instituted. If over 35 years of age, prophylaxis may or may not be necessary depending on the status of the immune system or other coexisting disease. This disease is not only treatable, it is 100% preventable.

THE KEY CAUSE

If we have to identify one causative factor for lung problems, it is smoking. The American Lung Association has estimated that smoking is the culprit for over 80% of chronic lung diseases, and it is responsible for the 2 million people with emphysema and 14 million with bronchitis.

Emphysema is probably one of the most debilitating diseases known to mankind. Once it has developed, it stays for life and disables and frustrates a person everyday of his life. Because there is no treatment available for this disease due to the destruction it brings to the lungs, the only measure doctors can take is to prevent complications or the progression of the disease. But there is good news - it may not be treatable but it is preventable!

What does smoking really do to a body?

There are about 410,000 deaths attributed to smoking each year. People who smoke less than half a pack a day have a death rate 30% higher than non-smokers, those who smoke 1-2 packs of cigarettes a day have a 100% greater risk of death, and those who smoke 2 or more packs per day, 140% higher. The World Health Organization estimates that there are about one billion smokers worldwide, with a death every 10 seconds or 3 million a year, about the same number as TB.

According to Andre Pasebecq of the Health Information Center, the following are the results of smoking:

a)   Heart – there are 10,000 times more heart contractions every day in a smoker's heart than a non-smoker.

b)   Heart Attacks – there are 3.3 times more risk of heart attack in smokers.

c)   Cancer – 146,000 deaths every year due to cancers caused by tobacco.

d)   Respiratory System – 98% of lung cancers are contracted by smokers.

e)   Vitamins – each cigarette burns up 2 mg. of Vitamin C.

f)   Stillbirths – 20% of babies are stillborn in mothers who smoke during pregnancy.

g)   Underweight babies – twice as many underweight babies are born to women who smoke during pregnancy.

h)   Impotence/frigidity – 90% of sufferers are smokers.

i)   Life Expectancy – each puff of a cigarette reduces the life expectancy by approximately one minute, which could amount to a total reduction of 8 to 22 years in one's lifetime.

What are the smoking-related cancers?

1. Cancer of the lung

2. Cancer of the esophagus

3. Cancer of the mouth and tongue

4. Cancer of the larynx

5. Cancer of the bladder

6. Cancer of the pancreas

7. Cancer of the uterus

8. Cancer of the cervix

In addition to cancer, what other problems are associated with smoking?

1. Stroke

2. heart disease

3. emphysema

4. chronic bronchitis

5. abnormal sense of taste and smell

6. stomach ulcer

7.　　high blood pressure

8.　　tachycardia　or increased heart rate

9.　　premature facial wrinkling

If smoking is so bad, how come the government does not make its manufacture and use illegal?

Are you kidding? And suffer the ire of the cigarette industry moguls, one of the most powerful groups of people on the face of the earth.

In the volume 4, number 7 issue of the *Journal of Longevity*, naturopathic doctor and fitness expert Bob Delmonteque shared his experiences with some of the biggest movie stars who were his clients. John Wayne smoked at least 5 packs of cigarettes a day and died of lung cancer. So did Yul Brynner and Robert Taylor. The others like Clark Gable, Tyrone Power and Errol Flynn also smoked and died of heart attacks.

In the recent past, smoking cigars has become more fashionable - with the mistaken belief that cigars are safer than cigarettes because they do not inhale, or inhale as deeply. However, researchers at UCSD have concluded that smoking a single large cigar is the same as smoking a whole pack of cigarettes. A cigar can contain as much as 70 times the amount of nicotine as a cigarette!

Second-hand smoke has the same toxins and cancer-causing elements as cigarettes. The National Cancer Institute has declared that one large, lighted cigar emits 20 times the ammonia as a cigarette and up to 90 times more cancer-causing nitrosamines.

In addition to cancer and heart disease, smoking produces other less deadly but perhaps equally frustrating diseases such as emphysema and male impotence. Emphysema is irreversible, while impotence can be treated and reversed. Smoking can cause damage to blood vessels and restrict blood flow to the penis, preventing erection. Dr. Charles Evans, professor of urology at the University of California at Davis, has called smoking the "most preventable cause of impotence."

Aside from the multitude of diseases that smoking brings about, it also accelerates the aging process. Each puff of a cigarette produces approximately 100 trillion free radicals that damage cells throughout the body, producing not only the different diseases already described, but also the less fatal conditions like visual problems and facial wrinkles. According to Dr. G. Ross in the article published in the *Journal of Longevity*, volume 4, number 2, the most devastating challenge is smoking "makes you dumber."

SECOND HAND SMOKE

How bad is secondhand smoke?

Dr. Lawrence Taylor defines secondhand smoke as "the exposure of non-smokers to tobacco combustion products in the indoor environment." He postulates that this is probably the third-leading preventable cause of death, behind direct smoking and alcohol abuse.

Passive, involuntary, secondhand smoke is a killer!

Living in a home with a smoker makes you inhale the smoke-laden breath of the smoker in addition to the smoke produced by the cigarettes polluting the indoor air. These people who suffer silently are subjected to an "almost two-fold risk of obstructive respiratory diseases over and above whatever risk is accorded by ambient air pollution in an urban environment" (Spitzer 1990).

The dangers of secondhand smoke are:
1) allergenic,
2) irritant,
3) toxic and
4) carcinogenic.

The Journal of the American Medical Association reported in the January 14, 1998 issue that there are 60,000 lives lost to secondhand smoke every year. About 11,000 adults were studied by a team of researchers from Wake Forest University, led by George Howard, and they found that secondhand smoke victimizes the arteries, with the carotids and coronaries as the most vulnerable producing plaques that lead to a stroke or a heart attack.

The National Cancer Institute has identified more than 4,000 individual compounds in tobacco and tobacco smoke, with about 200 known poisons (60 of which are known carcinogens or cancer-producing or cancer-enhancers). Among those compounds are: nicotine, carbon monoxide, tar, ammonia, phenols, cyanide, formaldehyde, benzene and nitrosamine.

WHY SMOKE?

Here are some disturbing statistics relating to smoking:

• It is now documented that sudden infant death syndrome (SIDS) is linked to maternal smoking. These mothers are also most likely to deliver babies that are underweight.

• Men who smoke produce damaged and fewer sperms. They possibly also father babies born with cancer.

• Smoking hurts not just the smoker but anyone exposed to him at home, at work or wherever he goes because of secondhand smoke.

•   Secondhand smoke from a parent increases a child's affinity for middle ear infection and asthma.

•   Secondhand smoke exposure of infants to 18 months old is associated with about 300,000 cases of respiratory infections.

•   In addition to the inflammation, cancers and breathing problems smoking produces, contrary to people's belief that it can calm their nerves, it actually produces the opposite effect because of the increased production of epinephrine, a hormone produced by the adrenals causing stress rather than relaxation.

Nicotine is the addictive substance in a cigarette. Each cigarette has about 6-11 mg. of nicotine and about 1-3 mg. per cigarette is absorbed. After inhalation, nicotine is absorbed into the bloodstream and the effect is felt within 8 seconds. A person with a habit of smoking a pack a day absorbs 20-40 mg. of nicotine daily. Double that for 2 packs a day.

According to M.D./alert Tips, after you stop smoking, your body starts to repair itself:

After...

- 20 minutes –blood pressure, heart rate and temperature of hands and feet become normal.

- 8 hours – nicotine and carbon dioxide blood levels cut in half; oxygen becomes normal.

- 1 day – the risk of heart attack begins to decrease. Carbon monoxide eliminated.

- 2 days – sense of taste and smell improves. Nerve endings start to grow. Mucus in airways break up and clear out lungs. Nicotine completely eliminated.

- 3 days – breathing easier. Bronchial tubes begin to relax and energy levels increase.

- 2 weeks to 3 months – circulation becomes better, breathing improves and walking becomes easier.

- 3-9 months – coughing, sinus congestion, shortness of breath and fatigue decrease; more energy. Lung function is increased by 10%.

- 1 year – risk of heart disease is now less than half than a year ago.

- 5 years – risk of cancer of the lung, mouth, throat and esophagus is half that of a pack-a-day smoker.

- 10 years – risk of dying of lung cancer is now similar to non-smokers.

- 15 years – risk of heart disease is the same as non-smokers.

HOW TO MANAGE LUNG DISEASES

The 3 main diseases that involve the respiratory system are:

1. cancer

2. chronic obstructive disease, i.e., emphysema

3. infection, like in pneumonia or bronchitis

Infection – this is probably the one disease that should be treated with prescription drugs namely, antibiotics, especially during the acute stages. If the infection is bacterial, the infection should respond easily to antibiotics, however, if the cause of the infection is non-bacterial like viral, then antibiotics do not do anything to slow it down or eradicate it.

Chronic obstructive disease, as in emphysema, has no known treatment in traditional medical practice. Most of the management is focused on prevention of complications. Infection is the most dreaded complication because breathing is so poor that any compromise in the breathing mechanism can tip patients into respiratory failure.

Even without infection, the most blatant symptom is difficulty in breathing, and patients need a constant oxygen supply to keep them going. This is especially true at night when they go to sleep, and sometimes even during the day when they are active.

The oxygen tension in their system is so low that physical activity is impossible to perform without aggravation of their breathing difficulty. Sometimes they are given bronchodilators to open up their airways, but these are usually not very helpful. There is also physical therapy through the tapping of the back of the patient at different positions, when that person is sometimes almost upside down, to help them expel the expectorations.

Cancer – the traditional treatment is in the form of surgery, radiation therapy or chemo-therapy, or a combination of two or three of them. Outside of these three treatments, traditional medicine has little new to offer. The discouraging part is when these are all followed, often the most optimistic predictions to prolong the life of the patient do not exceed five years. Sadly, the main cause of death in cancer patients is due to effect of their treatment, especially chemotherapy.

WHAT CAN ONE DO TO GET BETTER?

Obviously, the best scenario is the prevention of lung disease, and that can be accomplished quite easily. But, for people who already have the disease, there is hope.

For infection, there are a number of natural products that are available to fight it like echinecea, golden seal, colloidal silver or aloe vera.

For emphysema and bronchitis, or even asthma (chronic obstructive lung disease), intravenous hydrogen peroxide therapy is used. It is a good source of oxygen, and is a powerful antioxidant.

For cancer, management is directed at improving the immune system. The very first step is to change the diet to complete vegetarian, low salt, low fat with no dairy products.

Avoid sugar at all cost!

Take large amounts of antioxidants, especially Vitamin C. Manage stress. Take massive doses of intravenous Vitamin C. Intravenous peroxide therapy and intravenous polarizing solutions, ozone, pulsating magnetic field, hyperthermia and hypoglycemia are all alternative therapies used in many health centers, especially outside the United States, where there is more freedom of choice for patients.

Detoxification is also necessary and sometimes even chelation to remove heavy metal toxins.

CHAPTER SIX

6 CAUSE OF DEATH – ACCIDENTS

"Then the waters returned and covered the chariots, the horsemen, and all the army of Pharaoh that came into the sea after them...."
                                    Exodus 14:28

Accidents are the 6th cause of death, and are almost completely preventable.

According to the *New England Journal of Medicine* published in 1997, volume 337, number 8, injuries are the most common cause of death among people 1 to 34 years of age.

In 1994 statistics, there were 150,956 deaths from injuries. The U.S. Census Bureau reported a reduction in accidental deaths to 92,200 for 1997. Unintentional injuries accounted for 61% of the deaths, and nearly half of the unintentional injury deaths were due to motor vehicle accidents. In addition, 730 of the 807 bicyclists that died were injured in collisions with motor vehicles.

Falls, occurring primarily among the elderly, were the second cause of deaths from unintentional injuries. Poisonings were also cited as a significant cause of accidents and this was mainly due to unintentional overdoses of drugs. About equal numbers of people died from fires, scalding or drowning.

Intentional injuries were responsible for 56,100 deaths, of which 56% were due to suicide. Firearms accounted for 60% of suicides and 72% of homicides.

Injuries from motor vehicular accidents resulted in 43,900 deaths in 1995. Crashes are estimated to result in over 523,000 hospitalizations in the United States each year. Of the people killed in vehicular accidents, approximately 84% were occupants. About 41% of fatal injuries and 9 per cent of non-fatal injuries from motor vehicle crashes are associated with the use of alcohol.

Intoxicated drivers are more likely to have an accident because their driving skills are impaired, they are less likely to use seat belts and more likely to speed than sober drivers. The risk of fatal or non-fatal injury from a motor vehicle crash increases with the severity of the alcohol-related problems.

Seatbelts, which were introduced in 1968, have resulted in the reduction of the risk of serious injury or death by 45% in automobile accidents. The car seats for children reduced the risk by approximately 70%. In February, 2000, a very popular and much-loved football player from the Kansas City Chiefs, Derrick

Thomas, died from injuries sustained in a car accident a few weeks before. In that accident, there were two other passengers, one died instantly but the other one had only minor bruises and walked away. The one who survived was wearing his seatbelt while the two other passengers who died were not.

Air bags were designed as a restraint system that supplements seat belts in frontal collisions. Frontal air bags are estimated to reduce the risk of death by an additional 9% among belted drivers and by approximately 20% among unbelted, front-seat passengers.

Motorcycles are more dangerous than cars with a death rate per 100 million person-miles of travel of more than 35 times that of cars. Most serious or fatal injuries in motorcyclists involve the head. In one study, it was found that helmets decreased the risk of fatal head injury by 27%. Lower extremity fractures occurred in 52% of riders hospitalized with fatal injuries, and in 42% of those hospitalized with non-fatal injuries.

Use of illicit drugs or alcohol is more common among motorcycle riders involved in crashes, as compared with people in other types of motor vehicles, and substance abuse is more common among unhelmeted motorcyclists than among those who wore helmets.

WALK AND BIKE CAREFULLY

The first motor vehicle-related death in America involved a pedestrian in New York City in 1899. Injuries to pedestrians are the second largest category of motor vehicle deaths. The pedestrians most commonly injured are the very young (5 to 9 years of age), elderly and those intoxicated.

Bicyclists receive their share of injuries. Each year, there are approximately 800 deaths, 500,000 treated in the emergency rooms, and 1.2 million office or clinic visits attributable to bicycling. Head injuries account for about one-third of all injuries treated in emergency departments, two-thirds of hospitalizations, and three-fourths of deaths related to bicycling.

OTHER COMMON ACCIDENTS

The mortality and morbidity rates from falls are higher among the elderly than among younger people. Approximately 60% of persons who die from falls are 65 years old or older, and falls account for 87% of all fractures in older adults, the hip fracture being the most frequent consequence of falling. Osteoporosis is a significant predisposing factor in fractures in elderly women.

Poisoning is a cause of a significant amount of deaths in the United States. Solid or liquid poisons or drugs can be unintentionally ingested by children, or even adults, and cause morbidity or death.

Poisoning from domestic gas, as well as other sources of carbon monoxide, is another problem. Of the 11,547 unintentional deaths from carbon monoxide over a 10-year period, 575 were due to automobile exhausts. Since 1950 there has been an increase in reported poisonings, mainly because of overdoses to heroin and cocaine, and the use of medications by adults.

Fires kill. The main cause of death in 75% of residential fires is asphyxiation from smoke inhalation. Cigarettes are a major cause of residential fires. Smoke detectors have been shown to reduce the risk of death from residential fires by about 70%.

Drowning is another cause of mortality. Among children one to four years old, many drownings occur in swimming pools. Younger infants drown in bathtubs. There is a high prevalence of alcohol use – from 25 to 50% - of adults who drowned.

Firearms have been blamed in many violent deaths. There has been an increase in the propinquity of young people, ages 15 to 24 years, to homicides using a firearm. Firearms account for 60% of all suicides. Having firearms at home increases the incidence of both suicide and homicide.

HOW TO PREVENT ACCIDENTS

The treatment for accidents is to know what the main types of accident are, and by looking for ways to prevent them. There are three main categories of accidents which account for approximately two-thirds (67%) of all home accidents.

Impact accidents: These account for an incredible 55% of all home accident cases. Most are falls, but they also include being hurt by falling objects and general bumping-into-things type of accidents. The elderly are particularly at risk from falls of any kind.

Heat accidents: Injuries include scalds and burns. Burns are usually the result of contact from a controlled source such as a pot on top of a stove. Firemen tell us that the main sources of home fires each year are from cooking fat, misused and/or faulty appliances, wiring and smokers.

Mouth/foreign body accidents: This category includes accidental poisonings, suffocation, choking and objects in the eye/ear/nose. Children (0-4yrs) are especially vulnerable here as they are likely to put all manner of objects in their mouths.

To prevent these most common accidents, conduct a study to determine the current safety of your home. Check both upstairs and downstairs looking for worn and loose-fitting carpets, poor lighting - especially on stairs, unguarded fires, cracked plugs and worn flexes, furniture too close to fire places, etc.

WARNING! When carrying out this check do not put yourself at risk by messing with electrical wiring and appliances. Keep your fingers out of sockets.

Be vigilant.

With the help of your family, find out how to get out of your home quickly and safely in the event of a fire. Draw plans of your escape route, keep them and remember them. Of course, smoke detectors are imperative as an early warning system in case of fire.

Help the elderly in your home grow old – safely! As they get older, their physical abilities gradually change. They begin to move and react more slowly, and are less quick to see and avoid risks - particularly in homes where everything is so familiar and seems so safe. Elderly people often have accidents at home and these can be very serious indeed, sometimes fatal.

Again, do a safety check, making sure that grab bars are available in the necessary places, and that showers have non-slip surfaces.

Finally, if an unfortunate injury happens, the treatment mode is determined by what kind of injury and what systems of the body are involved.

CHAPTER SEVEN

7 CAUSE OF DEATH – DIABETES

"My son, give attention to my words; incline your ears to my sayings. Do not let them depart from your eyes; keep them in the midst of your heart; for they are life to those who find them, and health to all their flesh"
Proverbs 4:22-22

"It is not good to eat much honey..."
Proverbs 25:27

According to the *Forbes Magazine*, June 14, 1999 issue, the total number of patients in the U.S. afflicted with diabetes is about 15.7 million. The direct cost is about $44 billion annually, and another $54 billion for premature death and disability.

Diabetes Mellitus is the 7th cause of death in America, killing approximately 40,000 people each year. Globally, it has been projected that by the year 2025, there will be about 300 million afflicted with this disease and it will cause about 700,000 deaths a year. In addition, this disease will be a contributing factor in almost another 2 million deaths.

According to the 14th edition of *Harrison's Principles of Internal Medicine*, diabetes is the most common endocrine disease and is characterized by metabolic abnormalities and by long term complications involving the eyes, kidneys, nerves and blood vessels.

The most common symptoms are those secondary to hyperglycemia or elevated blood sugar, including frequent urination (polyuria), frequent drinking (polydipsia) and excessive swallowing (polyphagia). In the most severe cases, diabetic coma followed by death can be the presenting symptom.

Classification of Diabetes Mellitus:

1. Primary

   a. Autoimmune, type I, non-insulin-dependent diabetes mellitus

   b. Non-autoimmune, type 2, insulin-dependent-diabetes mellitus

2. Secondary

   a. Diabetes caused by pancreatic disease

   b. Diabetes caused by hormonal abnormalities

c. Drug or chemical-induced diabetes

d. Diabetes caused by insulin receptor abnormalities

e. Diabetes associated with genetic syndromes

f. Diabetes of other causes

There are approximately 800,000 new cases of diabetes diagnosed each year; and another 800,000 are asymptomatic and undiagnosed. Of these, about 95% are the non-insulin-dependent type. At the time of diagnosis, about 25% already have visual complications.

A BRIEF HISTORY

Diabetes first came into being around 1682 when a dog's pancreas was surgically removed, producing symptoms of diabetes (although it was not known as such then). The first clinical observation was made in 1775 when a certain Englishman discovered that there was not only elevation of blood sugar levels in diabetics, but there was also presence of sugar in the urine.

Three years later, abnormalities in the pancreas were described in patients with diabetes. At that point, diabetes had become a dreaded disease with no known treatment; long-term survival was impossible.

Before the end of the 18th century, starvation diets were the only accepted therapy. For over 100 years since, nothing much happened until 1921 when Banting and Best of Canada conducted experiments and produced insulin extracts from dogs. By 1922, extracts were being tested on human diabetic patients with resultant decreases in blood sugar levels. In 1923, Banting, the primary investigator, and Mcleod, his boss and the director of the laboratory where the work was done, received the Nobel Price for Medicine.

Since then, much progress has been achieved in the treatment of this once dreaded disease. Although numerous types of therapy have been accepted, the prospect of reversing this affliction through alternative medicine is something to be excited about. Moreover, diabetes is completely preventable.

THE DIAGNOSIS

To diagnose a case of diabetes mellitus, one or more of the following 3 criteria must be satisfied:

1) a fasting blood sugar level of at least 140 mg/dL on two occasions.

2) Symptoms of hyperglycemia with a random blood sugar level of at least 200 mg/dL.

3) Abnormal oral glucose tolerance test on two occasions.

PHYSIOLOGY

Insulin is produced by the beta cells of the pancreas whose main function is to facilitate the entry of glucose or sugar into the cells. Without insulin, the cells will not be able to give entry to the sugar which must then remain in circulation. In type II diabetes, where there is usually no shortage of insulin, because of the alteration in the receptors on the surface of the cells, insulin is unable to escort the sugar into the cells - giving rise to a medical problem widely known as insulin resistance. The result is the increasing presence of sugar in the blood which is then spilled in the urine. Obesity has been known to produce or exacerbate insulin resistance.

According to James Garvin III, M.D., Ph.D., of the Howard Hughes Medical Institute, type II diabetes is characterized by resistance to the action of insulin in target tissues, inadequate insulin production and secretion, or both. The organs and tissues that participate in the pathogenesis of the hyperglycemia of type II diabetes are those directly involved in endocrine control of plasma glucose. These are the triad of the beta cells of the pancreas, the liver, muscle and fat tissue. This triad controls sugar levels in a person with normal glucose metabolism.

The second portion of the small intestine, the jejunum, is responsible for the digestion of carbohydrates and the absorption of the resulting glucose into the bloodstream.

THE COMPLICATIONS

According to the *Consultations in Primary Care*, a supplement to the *Consultant*, volume 37, number 8, August 1997, diabetes is the country's leading cause of blindness, end-stage renal disease and lower-extremity amputations. Each year, about 20,000 diabetics become legally blind, another 20,000 develop renal failure and 54,000 undergo amputation. Of these amputations, 40% had amputations of the toe, 15% had amputations of the foot or ankle, 25% had amputations below the knee and another 20% had amputations above the knee.

In a study done in Rochester, Minnesota, diabetic neuropathy was present in 60-65% of patients with diabetes. The most common type was distal polyneuropathy, which affected about 45-55% of patients. Carpal tunnel syndrome was found in 35%, and autonomic neuropathy in 5-10%.

Cardiovascular complications are prevalent in diabetics. Coronary artery disease (CAD) is the most common complication found in patients with type II diabetes. Rates of CAD range from 30-50%, and are about twice the rates found in non-diabetic patients. Stroke is also twice as common in a diabetic as in non-diabetic patients.

The severest complication is, of course, premature death. Compared to the general population with a 1% death, 5.5% of diabetics die each year.

Risk factors for cardiovascular disease are also common in patients with type II diabetes. Hypertension is found in 50%, high cholesterol in 36%, high triglycerides in 25%, extreme obesity in 36%, and 20% smoke cigarettes. These are the risk factors for microvascular complications such as atherosclerosis and microvascular disease such as diabetic retinopathy, neuropathy or end-stage renal disease.

THE TREATMENTS FOR DIABETES

1.   Insulin – injection

2.   oral hypoglycemics – pills

3.   Natural products

4.   Diet

5.   Exercise

In medical practice, once a diagnosis of diabetes is made, treatment will usually consist of a diabetic diet, prescription oral medications to lower the blood sugar, or injections of insulin. Then the patient is followed in the office, and treatment is modified if necessary by using different brands of prescription drugs, or by changing the dose of the insulin, determining whether short-acting, immediate-acting or a long-acting insulin should be instituted.

In people practicing integrated medicine, there are other options in the form of natural health products like DiaBest (among others) which contain chromium, biotin and vanadium, all so crucial in the metabolism of carbohydrates. People have been known to stop their medications after they have used this product.

To prevent cardiovascular complications, chelation therapy is recommended. To prevent macular degeneration, an intravenous macular degeneration formula is used or there is an oral preparation called Super Vision that can also be used.

Obviously, diet and exercise are the mainstay in the management of diabetes. Exercises like walking should be done after each meal.

CHAPTER EIGHT

8 Cause of Death – Alzheimer's Disease

"For God has not given us a spirit of fear, but of power and of love and of a sound mind" 2 Timothy 1:7

"The memory of the righteous is blessed" Proverbs 10:7

Alzheimer's disease is the number eight cause of death in America, and is the most common degenerative disease of the central nervous system and the leading cause of dementia in the Western world.

Dr. Steven Gambert reported in *Postgraduate Medicine*, June 1977, that the youngest person diagnosed with this disease is 28 years old. Usually, this disease is found in elderly people; Alzheimer's disease is found in 5% of people over age 65 and 20-40% of people over age 80.

Alzheimer's disease was first described in 1907 by a pathologist, Alois Alzheimer, who noted changes in the neurohistology of middle-aged persons who had cognitive decline. Under the microscope, she noted plaques and neurofibrillary tangles in the brain with cortical neuronal loss, loss of dendrites, neuronal atrophy, and granulovascular degeneration.

Alzheimer's disease accounts for 50-60% of all cases of dementia.

This condition is characterized by progressive deterioration in intellectual function with increasing memory loss and personality changes that usually interfere with social and occupational activities. There could also be impairment of language ability, motor activities, recognition, and abstract thinking.

In an article published in the *Cortland Forum*, March, 1988, Dr. Krishan Gupta indicated that AD is an age-prevalent disease occurring in about 10% of people over 65 years of age; 25-40% of people over 85. Although dementia is seen mostly in adults, it should not be considered part of normal aging. It is estimated that a human brain contains about 20 billion neurons, and although loss of these cells may be considered part of aging, dementia should not be the end-result.

There are approximately 4 million Americans with dementia, and that number is expected to increase to 7 million by the year 2010.

Depending on symptoms, Alzheimer's disease is classified as follows:

1. <u>Mild</u> Alzheimer's disease is characterized by:

   • decline in short-term memory but not remote events

- misplacing objects

- forgetting names previously familiar

- trouble in finding words for familiar items

- inability to reach familiar locations

- loss of interest in surroundings

- inappropriate dressing for the weather

- deterioration of language skills

- deterioration of abstract thinking

- disorientation to time and place but not to person

- mini-mental score 20-25

- normal CT scan and MRI

2. Moderate Alzheimer's disease

- worsening memory

- behavioral problems (irritable, frustrated, argumentative)

- delusions and hallucinations

- mood swings

- wandering and pacing

- incontinence

- needs help in dressing, bathing, eating, etc.

- mini-mental score 12-20

- CT scan or MRI may be normal or with mild atrophy

3. <u>Severe</u> Alzheimer's disease

- increasing confusion and agitation

- delusion, hallucination

- paranoia

- incontinence

- poor mobility

- inability to communicate

- requires total help in daily activities

- mini-mental score <12

- more atrophy in CT scan or MRI

4. <u>Terminal</u> Alzheimer's disease (Steben Gambert, M.D., *Postgraduate Medicine*, June 1997)

- limited vocabulary (six words or less)

- absence of smiling

- inability to walk without assistance

- inability to sit up without assistance

- difficulty in eating or swallowing

- recent weight loss

- decreased consciousness or coma

- bowel or urinary incontinence

- recurrent respiratory or urinary tract infections

- inability to hold up head or follow objects with eyes.

There is no known cause for this unfortunate disease, although theories abound. There are scientists who believe that this is secondary to toxic material like aluminum, and others who believe that this may be related to lack of sleep. Others believe that this is secondary to deposition of amyloid in the brain.

The impact to society is tremendous with an estimated cost of close to $200,000 per person for lifetime treatment. Total cost in this country is approximately $100 billion annually.

THE TREATMENT

Treatment is mostly supportive since there are no specific drugs or procedures to cure this.

However, Alzheimer's disease is preventable!

In a study published in the British journal *Nature*, it was suggested that Alzheimer's disease could one day be treated or prevented by the use of a vaccine. The study worked on the idea of injecting a synthetic form of beta amyloid into mice, and after one year, the study found that the animals produced antibodies against the brain-clogging amyloid proteins. These antibodies triggered an immune response.

After dissecting the immunized mice, they found that 7 out of 9 had no detectable plaques in the brain. The conclusion is that the immune system was boosted up against the invading amyloid that prevented the disease from developing. This is precisely the crux of preventive medicine – to enhance the immune system so that disease of any kind will not develop.

In the case of Alzheimer's disease, there are certain measures that can be followed to increase the chances of avoiding its development.

For instance, since it has been said that lack of sleep could lead to memory loss, we should try our best to sleep at least 7 or 8 hours a day.

If all possible, these 7-8 hours should include the hours of 9 p.m. to 4 a.m. as it is during these hours that melatonin is at its maximum production.

In addition, one should follow a good exercise program to increase the production of neurotransmitters which are necessary in promoting good mental health.

Prescription medications are not curative for this kind of problem, but natural products such as Memo Rise, which is in capsule form, can be utilized to improve or prevent memory loss. This product has much to offer without the possibility of any side reactions. Continuously challenging the memory by keeping it active will also prevent memory challenges. The best form of mental exercise is by doing creative thinking and by reading.

Chelation therapy is most advantageous to these patients, especially if there is heavy metal toxicity or if the problem is circulatory. It would be most tragic if patients are just allowed to languish without trying this benign and probably beneficial treatment.

CHAPTER NINE

9 CAUSE OF DEATH – CORONARY ARTERY BY-PASS SURGERY

"Where there is no counsel, the people fall; but in the multitude of counselors there is safety." Proverbs 11:14

When a doctor pressures you to make a decision, or even makes remarks to make you think that if you do not go along with him, you will die – that is the time to pause and get at least another opinion. In cases of surgery, a second opinion must always be sought. A surgeon will normally lean towards doing a surgery rather than not doing it.

Remember, elective surgery can always wait.

THE BY-PASS SCENARIO

You are a middle-aged man or woman working in an office with other people. You have a responsible job which is relatively stressful. One Monday morning as you are going to your office, you suddenly feel some pressure on your chest and can hardly walk. After a few minutes, the pressure disappears and you feel alright.

That day you call your family doctor who examines you and recommends that you undergo a stress test, then a cardiac catheterization. But before the procedure is done, he will ask you to sign a consent form for the test. Often not explained to the patient, part of that consent form gives permission to allow open heart surgery "in case of an emergency."

There are two intense emotions that are paramount in a patient when listening to a cardiologist or a cardiac surgeon talk – fear and confusion. One is never at peace when there is discussion about heart surgery, especially when one is told that "you can drop dead anytime" or "you are a walking time bomb." Because of fear, any more elucidation creates a pile of confusion. When a decision for surgery must be made, the dialogue usually ends with the statement to the doctor giving permission to do surgery on yourself or a loved-one with, "Whatever you think is best, doctor!"

This is such an ironic situation because coronary by-pass surgery is supposed to prevent heart attack and death. Yet, it is one of the deadliest procedures ever invented by man!

PROVEN COMPLICATIONS

Depending on the hospital, the chances of dying from this procedure during surgery are between 1% to 20%, with most hospitals hovering at about 5%. Since there are about 500,000 (*Hospital Practice*, January 15, 1998) coronary by-pass surgeries done every year in the United States, deaths on the surgical table are astronomical. Using the 5% rate, at least 25,000 each year. These deaths do not include those who die after they have left the operating room. The saddest part of the entire process is that most people who suffer premature death in surgery probably did not even need the procedure since it is estimated that about 85% of these surgeries are unnecessary.

Dr. Rene Favoloro, one of the early pioneers of coronary artery by-pass grafting, in an article called *Landmarks in Development of CABG*, published in the August 4, 1998 issue of *Circulation*, pages 466-478, said "Coronary artery by-pass grafting is only a palliative treatment."

In the January 15, 1998 issue of the *Hospital Practice*, it claims that even when the operation is successful, it may not be the definitive solution, since coronary artery disease is a chronic disorder and the underlying atherosclerosis continues to progress.

Hospital Practice continues that atherosclerosis can affect both the native and grafted vessels. In fact, 10-20% of vein grafts are already occluded at hospital discharge after by-pass surgery. About 30% are completely occluded, and about 40% have significant occlusion at seven years post-surgery.

The patients receiving a 2nd, 3rd or 4th revascularization surgery have a recurrence rate of 50% within 2-3 years, and some with heart attacks.

In the November, 1997 issue of the *American Heart Journal*, pages 856-864, it states that percutaneous transluminal coronary angioplasty (PTCA) has overtaken the number of by-pass (CABG) surgery performed annually. The incidence of clinical restenosis or occlusion is 20-30% while the incidence of angiographic restenosis (occlusion) is 40-50%.

The three major complications of coronary by-pass surgery and angioplasty are: heart attack, stroke and death.

One of the less described but more serious complications of coronary by-pass surgery is memory impairment. In the issue of *Supplement II Circulation*, volume 96, number 9 on November 4, 1997, it reports that "Cognitive declines may persist in 5-35% of patients which may lead to long term changes in cognitive abilities."

The *Annals of Thoracic Surgery*, November 1997, pages 1287-1295, describes that the number of 3rd coronary artery by-pass operations is large enough to know that the in-hospital risks are greater than the first or second. In their study, 469 patients had a third by-pass surgery, and after 5 years, only 52% were alive.

According to Marcus Wellbourne, Science Editor for the *Gero Vita* newsletter, the highly touted by-pass surgery is a gold mine for doctors (and hospitals), but not for patients. Studies by Harvard Medical School researchers and the government's Office of Technology Assessment concluded that a whopping 85% of by-pass surgeries were not necessary.

Of those who receive a by-pass, over 80% are back within 7 years, in the same shape they were in before the surgery. In addition, 5% die during surgery (25,000 out of 500,000 surgeries); up to 19% (that's 95,000 people) have a heart attack, stroke or hemorrhage after surgery; almost 30% (150,000) have some brain damage; and another 20% (100,000) suffer severe depression, and many unhappy and frustrated men become impotent.

This is a $200 billion-a-year industry, and the most profitable among all the hospital services. If this surgery was reduced or eliminated, most hospitals would close.

As far as I am concerned, there are only two instances when a by-pass surgery should be done:

First, when there is almost complete occlusion of the left main coronary artery.

Second, when there is almost complete occlusion of a very proximal portion of the left anterior descending artery.

PREVENTATIVE PLANS

If coronary artery by-pass surgery is to be prevented, certain definitive measures should be adhered to strictly without increasing the possibility of a heart attack. They are as follows:

1. Stop smoking and stay away from places where there can be second-hand smoke.

2. Control weight to ideal.

3. Control high blood pressure.

4. Diet must not contain more than 10-15% of fat, and saturated fat must not be more than 10% of this. Going vegetarian with no dairy products is highly recommended. No eating of shellfish or fish with no scales or fins because of heavy metal toxicity.

5. Aerobic exercises – walking for 30 minutes a day.

6. Control the high cholesterol or high triglycerides – eat a lot of fibers or take encapsulated fibers like 60-Second Diet. Eating chicken without the skin is good because the fat is in the skin. However, cholesterol is in the meat. Because of this it may be necessary to take natural products that will reduce these substances

like Co-Less-Terol which has the same effect as the more commonly prescribed statin drugs. The difference is the former has no side effects, while the latter is fraught with very serious side effects.

7. Manage stress by modifying lifestyle. Studying and meditating on the Word of God is the best way to have peace (Philippians 4:6). Take some natural product that will give relaxation such as Stress Away.

8. Take antioxidants such as Cardio-Life.

9. Chelation therapy to remove toxic materials and improve circulation. Hundreds of thousands of people have been helped by this therapy. Symptomatic patients who have undergone by-pass surgery or patients scheduled for heart transplant have been tremendously helped by this therapy.

10. Rapha Oxidative therapy – this should be given along with chelation to improve oxygenation, enhance the immune system, and kill the organisms that may be present. There are now many reports incriminating infection as a precursor to plaque formation.

CHAPTER TEN

10 CAUSE OF DEATH – AIDS

"...I have set before you life and death, blessing and cursing; therefore choose life.." Deuteronomy 30:19

"...destruction comes like a whirlwind, when distress and anguish come upon you" Proverbs 1:27.

AIDS is the 10th cause of death in America. Just a few short years ago, this disease was not even in existence (or so we thought). But, as bad as it is that we have another disease to contend with, the disproportionate concern about this compared to other much more frequent causes of death seems incomprehensible.

For example, coronary by-pass surgery and drug reactions cause more deaths, yet people seem to accept them, resigned to that fact that they are a part of life, even though these abuses can be curtailed and prevented.

Contrary to popular thinking, HIV infection and AIDS did not just appear during the 70's, or even the flower generation of the 60's, but way before then. The accepted date of the first appearance of the HIV virus in a blood sample was in 1959.

The *Harrison's Book of Internal Medicine*, 14th edition, reports that AIDS was first recognized in the United States in the summer of 1981, when the Center for Disease Control and Prevention reported the unexplained occurrence of a strange lung disease called Pneumocystis carinii pneumonia in 5, and Kaposi sarcoma in another 26 previously healthy homosexual men.

Soon thereafter, this disease was recognized in intravenous drug users, in recipients of blood transfusions and in hemophiliacs. As the epidemiologic pattern became developed, it was concluded that an organism was responsible for the transmission of the disease by sexual contact, by intravenous means or by infected mothers to infants either intrapartum, perinatally, or via breast milk.

There is no evidence that HIV is transmitted by casual contact, or that the virus can be spread by insects, such as by a mosquito bite.

The HIV virus was isolated for the first time from a patient with enlarged lymph nodes in 1983. By 1984, it was clearly established that it was the causative agent of AIDS.

The report of February 2, 2000 by the Los Alamos National Laboratory, maintains that the deadly human immunodefeciency virus has been roaming the human population for at least 70 years. Some think it may even be as far back as five decades before that.

This virus apparently jumped from chimpanzees into humans sometime in the 1930's. How the virus transferred species is still a dilemma, although theories abound such as transmitting it from trapping or the eating of chimpanzees.

According to CARE Resource, AIDS is considered a terminal disease, killing thousands of men, women and an increasing number of children annually. The United States has the following statistical facts:

- AIDS is the leading cause of death for men 25-44.

- AIDS deaths among women have tripled in the past 10 years.

- More than half of the newly infected people are under 25 years old.

- Since 1996, at least 408,000 people Have tested positive for HIV, an increase of 270%.

- Florida is 3rd among States in AIDS cases, 73% of which are in Miami-Dade Broward and Palm Beach counties.

- It is projected that in 10 years, 10% of the population, or more than 34 million people, will be HIV-positive.

HOW TO TEST FOR AIDS
(from *Hospital Medicine*, July 1999, page 50)

Since the isolation of the human immunodeficiency virus in 1983, there have been two clinical tests that have proven very helpful in diagnosing HIV cases. These laboratory tests are for serum, saliva and urine antibodies for HIV. These tests are:

1. ELISA test or the enzyme-linked immunosorbent assay

2. WB or the Western Blot

Both of these tests are insensitive during the initial 3-4 weeks of infection. They first become positive about 22-27 days after acute infection.

Even though the ELISA test is used only for screening, in the past 3 years, its sensitivity has increased to 100%, and its specificity has been greater than 99.7%. The usual causes of false-positive reactions are Stevens-Johnson syndrome, syphilis, pregnancy, influenza immunization, severe liver diseases, chronic renal failure, hematologic malignancies, and various acute DNA viral infections.

False-negative reactions have been reported in patients with malignant or rheumatic disorders, bone marrow transplant recipients and immunosuppressive therapy.

Western block assays are used to confirm an ELISA- reactive serum as true positive. At the present time, WB achieves a sensitivity of greater than 99.2% and a specificity of 100%.

HOW TO PREVENT AIDS

What are the measures that can be implemented to prevent, or at least increase the chances of reversing AIDS?

1. Stay away from known factors that predispose you to contacting HIV infection, such as homosexual sexual activities, sharing infected needles, promiscuity, especially with unknown partners, prostitutes or otherwise.

2. Avoiding blood transfusions if at all possible.

3. Practicing safe sex by abstinence if not married, and by being faithful to your spouse if married.